M000169796

CHOCOLATE INDULGENCES

PHOTOGRAPHY AND DESIGN
BY KOREN TRYGG
TEXT BY LUCY POSHEK

ANTIOCH GOURMET GIFT BOOKS

Published by Antioch Publishing Company
Yellow Springs, Ohio 45387

ISBN 0-89954-827-X

CHOCOLATE INDULGENCES

Printed and bound in the U.S.A.

CONTENTS

A History of Chocolate

Certainly no chocolate lover today would question why *Theobroma*, the botanical name of the cacao tree, means "food of the gods." After all, aren't we forever comparing the taste of chocolate to a little slice of heaven?

The Aztecs were among the first to consume chocolate, and they regarded the cacao tree as truly divine. They believed that the seeds of the tree were brought to the earth by Quetzalcóatl, their Moon God. Aztecs who were lucky enough to reach eternal paradise presumably spent the rest of their days sipping chocolate drinks under cacao trees. Cacao beans were so valuable to this ancient civilization that they were used as currency.

The Aztecs processed the beans into a frothy, cold beverage called *xocoatl*, which means "bitter water." Thought to bestow exceptional energy and sexual prowess, this was the royal drink of Montezuma, the last Aztec emperor. He and his court managed to consume 2,000 cups of *xocoatl* a day.

In 1519, Hernán Cortés visited Montezuma's court and first tasted *xocoatl*. Although one of his soldiers commented that it "would be better thrown to the pigs than consumed by men," Cortés saw a more hopeful future in chocolate. He wrote, "A cup of this precious drink permits a man to walk for a whole day without food." He returned

to Spain in 1528 with a bounty of cacao beans and, more important, the knowledge of how to treat them.

The beans were taken to monasteries where the monks began to experiment with new methods—including the addition of cane sugar—to remove the bitterness from chocolate. As recipes were refined, the beverage grew so popular among the Spanish nobility that fashionable ladies began having chocolate brought to them in church during long services. Thought to strengthen the constitution, the drink also relieved many hungry stomachs during religious fasting periods.

Spain managed to keep the origin and preparation method of chocolate shrouded in secrecy for nearly one hundred years. Eventually, other European nations broke the monopoly by importing their own cacao beans. But high import duties kept chocolate out of reach to all but the very wealthy.

The Spanish princess, Anne of Austria, made chocolate a drink of the French court when she married Louis XIII in 1615. By the time Louis XIV succeeded him, a Royal Chocolate Maker to the King had been installed. The drinking of chocolate grew into such a grandiose ritual among the French royalty that those who were granted a visit to court began saying they had "gained admission to chocolate."

While fashionable chocolate houses were opening all over England and Holland in the early 1700's, colonial America was barely familiar with the substance. Finally, in 1765, James Baker and John Hannon converted an old Massachusetts grist mill into the first North American

cocoa factory. Baker's Chocolate is still the oldest American chocolate today.

During the nineteenth century, new technological advances enabled chocolate makers to transform the gritty beans into a smoother substance. In 1828, C. J. van Houten, a Dutch chemist, invented the cocoa press, which removed the cocoa butter from the beans. He also added alkali to remove acidity from the powder—still known today as Dutch process cocoa.

In 1847, Fry & Sons of England pioneered the first chocolate candies. Then, in 1875, Henri Nestlé, a Swiss chemist who had just invented condensed milk, teamed up with chocolatier Daniel Peter and created solid milk chocolate. Five years later, Rodolphe Lindt, also Swiss, invented "conching," a kneading process that made chocolate even smoother.

When Milton Hershey established the Hershey Chocolate Company in Pennsylvania in 1903, he had already developed a chocolate candy bar made from whole milk. Frank Mars took it one step further in the 1920's by adding layered centers to the candy bars.

Consumption of chocolate has increased dramatically in this century. Chocolate is now the number-one flavor choice in America. In fact, the average American consumes over nine pounds of chocolate per year. If that sounds like a lot, consider that the Swiss eat twenty pounds per year!

Evidently, most of us have a lot of catching up to do.

CHOCOLATE AND LOVE

The seductive powers of chocolate have been praised since ancient times. It was not without reason that Montezuma consumed up to fifty cups of it a day. Believing that chocolate increased his sexual prowess, he always drank a gobletful before entering his harem. (Considering that Montezuma had a harem of a thousand wives and concubines, perhaps he needed a little extra chocolate after all!)

It seems more than coincidental that chocolate candies —in heart-shaped boxes, no less—are traditional love tokens on Valentine's Day. And why are those delightful silver-wrapped chocolates called kisses? Do we associate chocolate with love simply because of the sensual pleasure its taste and texture evokes?

The fact that chocolate contains vitamin A, phosphorus, potassium, calcium, riboflavin, iron, niacin, and thiamine explains in part why it has always been considered revitalizing. This, plus its slight caffeine content, explains why soldiers, mountain climbers, and even astronauts rely on chocolate for quick energy.

As for the sexual claims, scientists have recently isolated small amounts of a substance in chocolate called *phenylethylamine*, which happens to be the same chemical produced in the brain when people fall in love. Nick-

named the "love drug," this chemical causes the endocrine glands to secrete hormones that offset depression and even make one feel slightly giddy.

While the "love drug" theory of chocolate is still under debate, one thing is certain: Chocolate has left a luscious trail of romantic tradition. Giving someone chocolate has always been considered an act of extravagance—especially when the chocolate comes in the exquisite form of velvety little truffles or chocolate-dipped fruit. On the other hand, a massive chocolate cheesecake will win anyone's heart, to be sure.

Chocolate-giving doesn't have to be sinfully expensive when you make the delicacy yourself. Present the love of your life with a chocolate torte baked in a heart-shaped pan; warm the body and soul with a steaming mug of hot chocolate à la Montezuma; even truffles are not as daunting to make at home as they used to be. Wrap a few of these exquisite morsels in cellophane and tie them up with a pretty ribbon. Even if your kitchen experiments come out looking imperfect, a handmade gift this special will surpass in gesture even the most expensive bon-bons, melting the heart of any chocolate lover.

There was a time, not so long ago, when Godiva chocolates could be delivered by a woman clad in a flesh-colored body stocking, atop a white horse, surrounded by minstrels...all for the tidy sum of $3,000.

TYPES OF CHOCOLATE

Cacao trees are now cultivated mostly in the equatorial regions of West Africa and South America. There are two main types of trees—criollo and forastero. Criollo beans are used for the finest chocolate and make up only ten percent of the world's production. Forastero beans, less delicate in flavor, supply the bulk of all chocolate.

The process from raw cacao beans to chocolate is a complicated one. The beans are first fermented, dried, roasted, and hulled. Then, because the resulting chocolate liquor is too rich in cocoa butter, most of the fat is extracted. The difference in chocolate types depends on how much cocoa butter was returned at the end of the process, plus whatever amounts of sugar, milk and other flavorings were added.

Unsweetened cocoa powder, used for baking, has all but about 10 percent of the cocoa butter removed.

Sweetened cocoa powder, used for making hot cocoa, contains nearly 25 percent cocoa butter and up to 80 percent sugar.

Dutch process cocoa powder has an even heavier cocoa butter content and slightly different flavor from other cocoas because of the small addition of alkali.

Unsweetened chocolate, which comes in solid squares

or cakes, contains 50 percent cocoa butter and no sugar or flavorings. It is used in baking and cooking.

Bittersweet and **semisweet chocolate**, also used in baking, both contain at least 35 percent chocolate liquor, plus cocoa butter, sugar and flavorings. Both types can be used interchangeably in recipes, but they vary from brand to brand. Bittersweet chocolate, used more in Europe, has a little less sugar than semisweet.

Sweet chocolate, which must have at least 15 percent chocolate liquor, consists mostly of cocoa butter, sugar and flavorings.

Milk chocolate is the same as sweet chocolate, only with milk solids added. About 90 percent of all chocolate consumed in the United States is milk chocolate, in the form of candy bars, icings, pies, and puddings.

White chocolate is not really chocolate at all because it contains no chocolate liquor—only cocoa butter, sugar, flavorings, and milk solids. It has a higher sugar content than dark chocolate and is difficult to melt.

Couverture refers to any professional-quality dipping or coating chocolate that has additional cocoa butter—32 to 39 percent—and is popular for dipping because of its shiny finish.

More than 240 million chocolate morsels are purchased every day in the United States.

CHOCOLATE TIPS

—One chocolate baking square is equivalent to one ounce.

—Before melting chocolate, chop it into coarse pieces or break it up in a food processor.

—Try not to use chocolate chips when recipes call for baking chocolate. Chocolate chips are not made to melt in the same manner.

—Although it is not ideal to use cocoa powder when a recipe calls for baking chocolate, it can be done: For 1

ounce of unsweetened baking chocolate, mix 3 tablespoons (2¼ Br. tbsp.) cocoa with 1 tablespoon (¾ Br. tbsp.) un-salted butter. Another 3 tablespoons (2¼ Br. tbsp.) sugar will make semisweet chocolate.

–All chocolate scorches easily, so melt it slowly over low heat. Two preferred melting methods are: in the top of a double-boiler, uncovered, over hot water; or in the microwave, uncovered–on medium for dark chocolate and low for milk chocolate. (Note: Microwaved chocolate will not visibly melt–you must stir it to see if it is melted.)

–Always use dry utensils when melting chocolate. Any moisture will cause chocolate to seize, turning it into a dull, thick paste.

–Do not add cold liquid to warm chocolate. Stir a few spoonfuls of the melted chocolate into the liquid so it can acclimatize before joining the chocolate mixture.

–Chocolate lasts a long time on the shelf–six months for milk chocolate and over a year for dark chocolate. It is best to store chocolate in a cool, dry place. If subject to too many temperature fluctuations, some of the cocoa butter will surface into a gray film called "bloom" that is harm-less but unattractive.

The melting point of cocoa butter is just below the human body temperature–that is why it literally melts in your mouth.

SINFUL CAKES

Chocolate cakes are so rich and moist, they often need no topping at all. True indulgence, however, calls for a crowning of velvety whipped cream, icing, fruit, or preserves. Dark chocolate cakes—especially tortes—can be easily decorated by placing a doily on top and sifting powdered sugar over them. When the doily is removed, you have a beautifully intricate white pattern.

Torte recipes generally use more eggs than traditional cakes, but less butter and flour. The egg yolks simulate the richness of butter while the egg whites provide the leavening of flour.

Chocolate Cheesecake Decadence

1½ cups (12 fl. oz.)
  chocolate wafers, crumbled
6 tbsp. (4½ Br. tbsp.) butter,
  melted
6 oz. semisweet chocolate
2 oz. unsweetened chocolate
32 oz. cream cheese, softened

1 tsp. (¾ Br. tsp.) vanilla
  extract
2 cups (16 fl. oz.) sugar
4 eggs
1½ cups (12 fl. oz.) sour
  cream
¾ cup (6 fl. oz.) semisweet
  chocolate chips

Break semisweet and unsweetened chocolate into pieces. In a small saucepan over low heat, melt the chocolate, stirring until smooth. Let mixture cool.

Combine wafer crumbs and butter. Press in bottom and 2 inches up the sides of a 9-inch springform (loose bottom) pan. Set aside.

Preheat oven to 350°F. In a large mixing bowl, beat cream cheese and vanilla with an electric mixer until fluffy. Gradually beat in sugar. Add eggs one at a time, beating until just blended. Stir in sour cream. Add the melted chocolate and mix until well blended. Fold in the chocolate chips. Pour mixture into the prepared crust. Bake 50 to 60 minutes until cheesecake begins to crack at edges and the center is firm. Turn off oven. Cool cheesecake in oven with door ajar for 1 hour; then chill thoroughly, ideally overnight. Remove sides of pan before serving. Garnish with whipped cream if desired. Serves 10 to 12.

Chocolate-Raspberry Dream Cake

Cake

2 cups (16 fl. oz.) cake flour
1¾ cups (14 fl. oz.) sugar
¾ cup (6 fl. oz.) cocoa powder
1¼ tsp. (1 Br. tsp.) baking soda
1 tsp. (¾ Br. tsp.) salt
½ tsp. baking powder
1¼ cups (10 fl. oz.) milk
¾ cup (6 fl. oz.) butter
3 eggs
1 tsp. (¾ Br. tsp.) vanilla

Frosting

2 cups (16 fl. oz.) heavy whipping cream
½ cup (4 fl. oz.) powdered (icing) sugar
2 tbsp. (1½ Br. tbsp.) unsweetened cocoa powder
6 tbsp. (4½ Br. tbsp.) raspberry jam

Preheat oven to 350°F. Grease and flour 3 round 9-inch cake pans. In a large mixing bowl place all the cake ingredients. Beat with an electric mixer on low speed until well mixed, then beat for 5 minutes at high speed. Pour batter into pans. Stagger pans on 2 oven racks so that no pan is directly above another. Bake

20 to 30 minutes or until toothpick placed in center comes out clean. Cool pans on wire racks for 10 minutes; remove layers from pans and cool them on wire racks for 2 hours.

In a chilled mixing bowl, beat whipping cream until fairly stiff. Add powdered sugar and cocoa powder and beat until cream has stiff peaks. Place one cake layer on a platter; spread half the raspberry jam and some of the whipped cream on top. Repeat with the next layer; then frost top and sides with the remaining whipped cream. Coat the top and sides with shaved chocolate curls or garnish with raspberries if desired.

"Few pleasures are greater than turning out a perfect cake...Such creations can bring happiness to both our childhood and mature years, for few, if any, people are immune to their charm, and memories of them...lighten the dark corners of life."

JOSEPH AMENDOLA

AND

DONALD LUNDBERG

Chocolate Almond Torte

Torte

6 oz. semisweet chocolate
5 oz. butter
8 eggs, separated
1 cup (8 fl. oz.) sugar
1 tbsp. (¾ Br. tbsp.) crème de cacao or amaretto
⅔ cup (5⅓ fl. oz.) flour
⅔ cup (5⅓ fl. oz.) ground almonds
¼ cup (2 fl. oz.) black cherry preserves
sliced almonds for decoration

Glaze

6 oz. semisweet chocolate, broken into bits
½ cup (4 fl. oz.) sugar
¼ cup (2 fl. oz.) light corn syrup
3 tbsp. (2¼ Br. tbsp.) butter
1 tsp. (¾ Br. tsp.) vanilla extract

Preheat oven to 350°F. Grease and lightly flour two 9-inch cake pans. In a medium pan over very low heat, melt chocolate and butter, stirring until mixture is smooth. Remove from heat; cool. Beat egg yolks until thick; add to chocolate mixture. Stir in liqueur; set aside. In a large mixing bowl, beat egg whites with electric mixer on medium speed until soft peaks form.

Slowly add sugar, beating at high speed until stiff peaks form. Stir a third of the egg whites into the chocolate mixture. Pour the egg-chocolate mixture over the remaining egg whites. Sprinkle the flour and ground almonds over the mixture; carefully fold mixture together just until blended. Transfer batter to prepared pans. Bake 20 minutes or until toothpick placed in center comes out clean. Cool in pans on wire racks for 10 minutes. Remove from pans. Cool cakes on wire racks for 2 hours.

While the cakes are cooling, melt chocolate with sugar and corn syrup in a medium pan over low heat, stirring frequently. Bring mixture to a low boil and cook 3 to 4 minutes, stirring occasionally. Mix in the butter and vanilla; then remove from heat. Let cool before glazing torte.

To assemble the torte, place one cake layer on a serving plate. Spread cherry preserves over top; add second layer. Spread glaze over top and sides. Decorate sides of cake with sliced almonds.

"Once in a young lifetime one should be allowed to have as much sweetness as one can possibly want and hold."
JUDITH OLNEY

DIVINE TRUFFLES

Truffles are the most luxurious items in any confectioner's shop. These little balls of rich, velvety chocolate may appear in an assortment of coatings such as chopped nuts or cocoa powder. Often elegantly packaged, truffles may seem inaccessible to the average cook; but they are surprisingly easy to make at home.

Many truffles enclose a separate center called a *ganache*, which is made out of chocolate, butter or cream, and flavorings. Ganache can be made ahead of time and refrigerated; then it is shaped into balls and frozen until ready for dipping.

Melting chocolate for dipping can be the trickiest step of truffle-making. Some purists insist that the chocolate needs to be tempered—a complicated procedure which gives the chocolate a long-lasting smooth gloss and protects the surface from getting a "bloom" of gray film. But if you plan to refrigerate your truffles and consume them in short order, tempering is unnecessary.

Nonetheless, chocolate-melting must be done carefully and slowly (see Chocolate Tips). Most important, never allow any moisture to come in contact with chocolate—not even a drop of water—or it can seize into a useless paste. Humid weather can also adversely affect chocolate. Try to

make truffles on a cool, dry day.

Dipping the frozen ganache in the melted chocolate is sometimes done with a dipping fork. After dipping, the truffle is gently slipped onto waxed paper in an inverted position, with any leftover chocolate swirled over the top. In the absence of a dipping fork, simply roll each ganache by hand in the melted chocolate.

Black Velvet Macadamia Truffles

4 oz. fine-quality semisweet chocolate, broken into bits
3 tbsp. (2¼ Br. tbsp.) heavy cream
1 tbsp. (¾ Br. tbsp.) powdered (icing) sugar
1 tbsp. (¾ Br. tbsp.) crème de cacao or rum
⅓ cup (2⅔ fl. oz.) macadamia nuts, finely chopped
1 tbsp. (¾ Br. tbsp.) ground macadamia nuts (opt.)

In a small saucepan over very low heat, melt chocolate with heavy cream, stirring until smooth. Pour mixture into a mixing bowl. Add powdered sugar and beat with an electric mixer for 8 minutes until thick. Add the liqueur and beat 2 minutes longer. Stir in the chopped nuts; cover and chill. Shape chocolate into ½-inch balls. Roll in ground nuts to coat if desired. Refrigerate or freeze until ready to serve.

Mocha Truffles

6 oz. semisweet chocolate, cut into bits
2 tbsp. (1½ Br. tbsp.) strong black coffee
2 tbsp. (1½ Br. tbsp.) cream
1½ tbsp. (1 Br. tbsp.) coffee-flavored liqueur
2 tbsp. (1½ Br. tbsp.) unsweetened cocoa powder

Melt chocolate, coffee and cream in a double boiler over hot water. Stir well. Pour mixture into bowl and beat with an electric mixer for 10 minutes until thick. Add liqueur and beat 2-3 minutes longer. Cover and chill.

Shape chocolate into ½-inch balls. Roll in cocoa powder until evenly coated. Refrigerate or freeze until ready to serve.

Crème de Menthe Truffles

6 oz. semisweet chocolate, cut into bits
4 tbsp. (3 Br. tbsp.) butter, cut into bits
3 tbsp. (2¼ Br. tbsp.) heavy cream
3-4 tbsp. (3 Br. tbsp.) crème de menthe as desired
1 lb. semisweet chocolate (for dipping)
2 tbsp. (1½ Br. tbsp.) unsweetened cocoa powder (opt.)

*I*n a heavy medium saucepan combine the chocolate, butter and cream. Stir frequently over low heat until chocolate is melted. Pour mixture into a bowl and beat with an electric mixer for 10 minutes until thick. Add crème de menthe and beat 2 to 3 minutes more. Pour into a clean bowl; cover and chill until firm, about 4 hours.

Quickly shape chilled chocolate into ½-inch balls (ganache). Place balls on a pan and freeze until firm.

Melt the dipping chocolate in the top of a double boiler or in a microwave oven, stirring frequently until smooth. Then, wiping moisture from the bottom of the saucepan, pour the chocolate into a shallow pan. Line another pan with waxed paper and arrange all three pans (frozen centers included) closely so they are in order. Working quickly and leaving one hand clean, roll the frozen chocolate centers in the melted chocolate and place them on the waxed paper to dry. Then roll them in cocoa powder if desired. Store truffles immediately in the refrigerator to set coating, then remove to a covered container for storage. Makes about 48 truffles.

"I feel the end approaching.
Quick, bring me my dessert, coffee, and liqueur."
PIERETTE BRILLAT-SAVARIN'S *last words*

HEAVENLY MOUSSES

There is nothing like a luxurious, velvety mousse to bring out the best in fine chocolates. The flavor is further enhanced when it is prepared in advance and kept in the refrigerator for a day or two.

The key to a good mousse is proper folding. Also, make sure all the ingredients are the same temperature and nothing is overwhipped.

Chocolate Mousse with Raspberries

4 oz. fine-quality semisweet chocolate
2 eggs, separated
¾ cup (6 fl. oz.) whipping cream, chilled
4 tbsp. (3 Br. tbsp.) powdered (icing) sugar
1 tbsp. (¾ Br. tbsp.) crème de cacao or brandy
fresh raspberries
freshly whipped cream with sugar to taste
grated chocolate

In a medium saucepan over low heat, melt chocolate, stirring frequently. Let cool. Beat egg yolks until thick. Add to melted chocolate, stirring well. In a large bowl, beat egg whites, gradually adding powdered sugar until stiff peaks form. In a separate bowl, whip the cream until stiff peaks form. Add a scoop of egg white to the chocolate yolk mixture. Stir until smooth. Add this mixture to the rest of the egg whites and mix until well blended. Stir in the crème de cacao or brandy. Fold in the whipped cream until just blended. Cover bowl and chill several hours or overnight.

Assemble clear dessert glasses. Spoon a layer of mousse into each glass. Add a layer of fresh raspberries and another layer of mousse. Top with whipped cream and garnish with additional raspberries and grated chocolate. Serves 4 to 6.

Chocolate-Orange Mousse
in Chocolate Cups

Mousse

1 tsp. (¾ Br. tsp.) unsweetened cocoa
1 tsp. (¾ Br. tsp.) strong coffee or espresso
¼ cup (2 fl. oz.) boiling water
7 oz. bittersweet or semisweet chocolate
4 tbsp. (3 Br. tbsp.) sweet butter, cut into pieces
4 eggs, separated
¾ cup (6 fl. oz.) sugar
3 tbsp. (2¼ Br. tbsp.) orange-flavored liqueur
grated rind of one orange
½ cup (4 fl. oz.) heavy cream
½ tsp. salt

Cups

6 oz. semisweet chocolate
1 tbsp. (¾ Br. tbsp.) butter

Dissolve cocoa and coffee in boiling water and pour into top of double boiler. Add chocolate and melt over simmering water. Then add butter, bit by bit, beating with a wire whisk until each piece is dissolved.

In mixing bowl, beat egg yolks and sugar with an electric mixer until thick. Add chocolate mixture, continuing to beat. Then beat in liqueur and grated orange rind. In separate bowl, beat cream until thick. Gently fold into chocolate mixture. In third bowl, beat

31

egg whites and salt until stiff, then fold last into chocolate mixture. Chill 4 to 24 hours.

Meanwhile, place fluted paper muffin cups in a
medium-sized muffin tin. Melt chocolate and butter
over hot water, stirring until mixture is smooth. Drizzle
melted chocolate down the sides of each paper muffin
cup, one heaping teaspoonful at a time, covering sides
evenly. Chill chocolate cups until firm.

Before serving, carefully peel paper from each cup.
Place chocolate cups on a chilled platter and fill them
with mousse. Garnish with candied orange slices if
desired.

DELECTABLE COOKIES

In 1930, Ruth Wakefield
invented the chocolate chip cookie—using chopped-up
pieces of a chocolate bar—at her Massachusetts restaurant,
the Toll House Inn. They caught on so fast that when
Nestlé noticed a dramatic increase in the sales of their
semisweet chocolate bars, they decided to investigate.
Their invention of chocolate chips, or morsels, soon fol-
lowed.

Americans now bake more than seven billion chocolate
chip cookies per year. Thus, no chocolate book would be
complete without yet another variation on this cookie
classic.

Chocolate Chocolate-Chip Cookies

2 cups (16 fl. oz.) all-purpose flour
¼ cup (2 fl. oz.) sweetened cocoa powder
1 tsp. (¾ Br. tsp.) salt
1 tsp. (¾ Br. tsp.) baking powder
1 tsp. (¾ Br. tsp.) cinnamon
¼ tsp. powdered cloves
1 cup (8 fl. oz.) butter, softened
1½ cups (12 fl. oz.) packed brown sugar
2 eggs
1 tsp. (¾ tsp.) vanilla
1½ cups (12 fl. oz.) semisweet chocolate chips
macadamia nuts, chopped (opt.)

Preheat oven to 375°F. Combine first six ingredients in a bowl and set aside. In large bowl, cream together butter and brown sugar. Beat in eggs and vanilla. Gradually add flour mixture, chocolate morsels, and macadamia nuts, if desired. (Dough should be stiff; add more flour if necessary.) Drop by the spoonful on ungreased cookie sheets. Bake 8 minutes. Makes about 5 dozen cookies.

Double Fudge Brownies

2½ oz. butter
2 oz. unsweetened chocolate
1¼ cups (10 fl. oz.) sugar
2 eggs
1 tsp. (¾ Br. tsp.) vanilla
  extract

½ cup (4 fl. oz.) flour
½ cup (4 fl. oz.) semisweet
  chocolate chips
½ cup (4 fl. oz.) chopped
  nuts (opt.)

Preheat oven to 350°F. Grease an 8-inch square pan. In a medium saucepan over low heat, melt the butter and unsweetened chocolate, stirring to blend. Remove from heat; let cool about 5 minutes. Stir in the sugar, then the eggs and vanilla until well mixed. Add the flour and stir just until blended. Fold in the chocolate chips and chopped nuts. Spread in pan. Bake about 25 minutes until edges pull away from sides of pan. Cool in pan on wire rack at least 20 minutes before cutting into squares.

LUSCIOUS BEVERAGES

It was during the Renaissance that chocolate changed from a cold to a hot drink. Chocolate pots were invented with a hole in the lid through which a swizzle stick extended. The chocolate was whipped into a froth and taken in tall, narrow cups that best retained heat.

Since then, many countries have created their own variations on the serving of hot chocolate: **French chocolate** has a base of milk and cream; **Viennese chocolate** is topped with whipped cream or *schlag*; **American hot chocolate** traditionally has a marshmallow topping; **Russian chocolate** and **Brazilian chocolate** include coffee; **Mexican chocolate** contains cinnamon and sometimes orange rind.

When making chocolate beverages, keep in mind that cocoa powder does not always mix easily with liquid. One way to avoid lumps is to remove them before cooking, or, if sugar is being used, mix the cocoa and sugar together first.

Like hard chocolate, cocoa scorches easily, so do not bring it to a hard boil. Just before serving, whip the liquid with a whisk to prevent the "skin" that so often appears at the top.

Thomas Jefferson once declared the hope that "the superiority of chocolate, both for health and nourishment, will soon give it the same preference over tea and coffee in America which it has in Spain."

35

Cocoa of the Gods

3 1½ oz. milk chocolate candy bars, broken into bits
1½ cups (12 fl. oz.) whole milk
whipped cream
chocolate wafer cookies, crushed

P̶lace chocolate pieces in a small saucepan and melt over lowest heat setting, stirring constantly. Slowly pour in milk and continue stirring until mixture is smooth. Raise temperature to medium and continue cooking until cocoa is hot, approximately 1 minute. Serve in mugs. Garnish with whipped cream and cookie crumbs. Serves 2.

Chocolate Soda Supreme

¼ cup (2 fl. oz.) chocolate syrup
½ cup (4 fl. oz.) cold milk
4 to 6 scoops dark chocolate ice cream
club soda or 7-Up
whipped cream, chocolate shavings and cherries

Mix milk with chocolate syrup. Pour into two tall glasses. Add one scoop of ice cream to each glass. Pour in a small amount of soda. With the back of a long-handled spoon, mix ice cream, chocolate milk and soda together. Add another one or two scoops of ice cream to each glass. Fill glasses with soda. Garnish with whipped cream, chocolate shavings and cherries if desired.

Chocolate Moose Milk

½ cup (4 fl. oz.) coffee
⅓ cup (2⅔ fl. oz.) vodka
¼ cup (2 fl. oz.) crème de cacao

chocolate ice cream
ice cubes

Pour coffee, vodka, and crème de cacao into a blender. Fill blender halfway to the top with chocolate ice cream and ice cubes. Blend mixture and pour into two tall glasses.

(Note: You may want to take it to bed and drink it there!)

MORE WICKED INDULGENCES

Fortunately for chocolate lovers, the "food of the gods" goes well with, and is usually enhanced by, a multitude of flavors. Mint, coffee, nuts, and liqueurs are only a few of chocolate's best complements. Ice cream of any flavor is never better than with chocolate dribbled or sprinkled on top. And what chocolate does for fruits such as raspberries, cherries and oranges is at the very least sublime.

Chocolate Cherry Bombs

Drain the liquid from a jar of maraschino cherries and replace the liquid with vodka. Allow the cherries to soak for 30 to 60 days.

When the cherries are thoroughly "marinated," cut a bar of fine-quality semisweet dipping chocolate into bits (or grate it in a food processor). Melt the chocolate in the top of a double boiler, stirring frequently. Remove pan from heat. Holding the cherries by their stems, dip them one by one in the melted chocolate. Let the cherries cool on a sheet of foil; freeze them for 10 minutes, then store in the refrigerator until ready to serve.

Old-Fashioned Chocolate Ice Cream Pie

2 oz. unsweetened chocolate
2 tbsp. (1½ Br. tbsp.) butter
2 tbsp. (1½ Br. tbsp.) hot milk or water
⅔ cup (5⅓ fl. oz.) sifted powdered (icing) sugar
1½ cups (12 fl. oz.) snipped coconut
½ gallon (64 fl. oz.) chocolate ice cream

Melt chocolate and butter in the top of a double boiler. Stir in milk and powdered sugar, then coconut. Press mixture with the back side of a spoon into the bottom and sides of a greased 8-inch pie pan. Refrigerate crust and remove 15 minutes before serving to fill with ice cream. Can garnish with grated chocolate, chocolate shavings, or Grandma's Chocolate Sauce (see below) if desired.

Grandma's Chocolate Sauce

1 cup (8 fl. oz.) sugar   ½ cup (4 fl. oz.) water
2 oz. semisweet chocolate

Stir sugar and water in saucepan while mixture comes to a boil. Add chocolate and simmer for 5 minutes, stirring often. Serve warm or cold over ice cream.
    (This sauce will have an old-fashioned granular texture unlike most other chocolate sauces.)

Chocolate Cream Tiramisu

16 ladyfingers
⅓ cup (2⅔ fl. oz.) Irish Cream liqueur
¼ cup (2 fl. oz.) chocolate syrup
5 eggs, separated
1½ cups (12 fl. oz.) powdered (icing) sugar
8 oz. mascarpone cheese, softened
2 tbsp. (1½ Br. tbsp.) unsweetened cocoa powder

*A**rrange ladyfingers on the bottom of a square or oval 2-inch-deep serving dish. Pour Irish Cream liqueur and chocolate syrup evenly over ladyfingers.*

*Set aside. In a mixing bowl, cream egg yolks and pow-
dered sugar with an electric mixer. Add mascarpone
cheese and beat until smooth. In a separate bowl,
whip egg whites until stiff. Stir a quarter of the whites
into mascarpone cheese mixture to lighten. Quickly
fold in remaining egg whites. Spread mascarpone mixture over ladyfingers. Sift cocoa powder over the top
and refrigerate covered for 1 to 2 hours. Serves 6 to 8.*

*(Cream cheese may be substituted for mascarpone
cheese.)*

Chocolate Soufflé with Amaretto Sauce

Soufflé

3 tbsp. (2¼ Br. tbsp.) butter
2 oz. unsweetened chocolate
3 tbsp. (2¼ Br. tbsp.) flour
1¼ cups (10 fl. oz.) milk
1 tbsp. (¾ Br. tbsp.) amaretto
⅓ cup (2⅔ fl. oz.) sugar
4 egg yolks
6 egg whites

Amaretto Sauce

½ cup (4 fl. oz.) heavy cream
¼ cup (2 fl. oz.) sugar
1 oz. semisweet chocolate
1 tbsp. (¾ Br. tbsp.) butter
2 tbsp. (1½ Br. tbsp.) amaretto

*P*reheat oven to 400°F. Place the rack very low in the oven. Butter 8 3½ oz. ramekin cups and sprinkle the insides evenly with sugar.

Melt the butter and chocolate in the top of a double boiler. Add the flour, whisking until smooth. Whisk in the milk and amaretto. Move pan from double boiler to burner and raise heat. As the mixture starts to thicken, gradually whisk in the sugar. Cook until just boiling and thick, stirring constantly to prevent scorching. Remove pan from heat and allow to cool slightly.

Whisk egg yolks into chocolate mixture one at a time. In a mixing bowl, beat the egg white until fairly stiff but not dry. Stir one fourth of the egg whites into the chocolate mixture. Then quickly fold in the remaining whites until the mixture is smooth. Fill each ramekin almost to the top. Bake up to 15 minutes, until each soufflé is puffy, delicately crusty on top, and slightly wet inside.

While soufflés are baking, combine the cream, sugar, chocolate, and butter in a small saucepan, stirring over low heat until smooth and mixture has thickened. Remove the pan from heat and stir in the amaretto. When soufflés are done, serve them immediately in their cups with a bowl of amaretto sauce on the side.

Really Fudgy Ice Cream

1½ cups (12 fl. oz.) light cream
1 cup (8 fl. oz.) heavy cream
¾ cup (6 fl. oz.) sugar
4 egg yolks

6 oz. semisweet
   chocolate, grated
1 tbsp. (¾ Br. tbsp.)
   vanilla extract

In a medium saucepan over medium heat, bring the creams and ½ cup (4 fl. oz.) sugar to a low boil; remove from heat. In a bowl, beat the egg yolks and remaining ¼ cup (2 fl. oz.) sugar until thick. Add a quarter of the cream mixture to the yolks and blend well. Return the mixture to the pan. Continue cooking over medium heat, stirring constantly until custard-like, 4 to 5 minutes; remove from heat. Mix in the chocolate. Let cool. Stir in the vanilla. Cover and refrigerate at least 1 hour, stirring occasionally until well chilled.

Scoop the custard mixture into an ice-cream maker and freeze according to manufacturer's instructions. After ice cream has been churned, pack in covered container and freeze. Makes 1 quart.

*"I doubt whether the world holds for anyone
a more soul-stirring surprise than the
first adventure with ice-cream."*

HEYWOOD BROUN

Sundae in the Dark

In an oversized dessert dish, place an oversized Double Fudge Brownie (recipe on page 34). Directly on top, place scoops of Really Fudgy Ice Cream (recipe on page 43). Drizzle with Fudge Sauce Rhapsody (recipe on page 45). Top with dollops of Whipped Cream Ecstasy (recipe on page 45).

"Give me chocolate, or give me death."

The Joy of Pigging Out

Fudge Sauce Rhapsody

¼ cup (2 fl. oz.) sweetened condensed milk
¼ cup (2 fl. oz.) whipping cream
1 oz. semisweet chocolate, grated

Mix condensed milk and cream in a saucepan. Add the grated chocolate. Over medium heat, bring the mixture to a boil, stirring frequently. Reduce to low heat, stirring frequently until sauce thickens, 5 to 10 minutes.

Whipped Cream Ecstasy

½ cup (4 fl. oz.) heavy cream
2 tbsp. (1½ Br. tbsp.) sugar
2 tsp. (1½ Br. tsp.) light crème de cacao
1 oz. fine-quality milk chocolate, grated

Pour well-chilled cream in a mixing bowl. With an electric mixer on medium speed, beat cream until soft peaks form. Add sugar and beat on high speed until stiff peaks form. With a wire whisk, beat in crème de cacao, then grated chocolate. Dollop on Sundae in the Dark, other desserts, coffee, or cocoa.

DELIGHTFUL GARNISHES

To make grated chocolate: Use a food processor (in which case it is best to use semi-sweet or bittersweet chocolate) or a hand grater. Grated chocolate can be sprinkled on top of cakes, pies, tortes, custards, and ice cream.

To make shaved chocolate: Hold a wrapped bar of unsweetened or semisweet chocolate in your hand to warm it slightly. Shave the bar in short, quick, irregular strokes with a vegetable peeler or small sharp knife, holding it over a plate to catch the shavings.

To make chocolate curls: Follow the same procedure as for shaved chocolate (though milk chocolate is preferable for curls), but use long, careful strokes instead. Shave the narrow end of the bar for thin curls, the flat side for wide curls. Curls can garnish a torte, cake or cheesecake.

To make chocolate leaves: Melt two ounces of bittersweet or semisweet chocolate and stir until smooth. Cool until glossy. Brush the melted chocolate on the underside of dry, nontoxic leaves such as mint or lemon. Build up several layers of chocolate. Place them on waxed paper to set. When firm (they can be hardened in the refrigerator), peel the real leaf away, starting at the stem. Three ounces of melted chocolate will coat six small leaves.

*"It flatters you for a while.
It warms you for an instant.
Then all of a sudden, it kindles a mortal fever in you."*

MADAME DE SÉVIGNÉ, *on chocolate*

GRAPHIC DESIGN BY GRETCHEN GOLDIE

PHOTO STYLING BY SUE TALLON

ACKNOWLEDGMENTS

CHARLIE BARR; RUTH HANKS;
BRAD, LYNNE, BETH, KATIE AND TOM HENNING;
DEBORAH JOYCE; ALMA MEIERDING; REBECCA SEGAL;
LINDA, JULIE AND ANDREW TRYGG; GWEN VAN LOOS.